Who Shall Be the Sun?

Who Shall Be the Sun?

POEMS BASED ON THE

LORE, LEGENDS, AND MYTHS

OF NORTHWEST COAST AND

PLATEAU INDIANS

David Wagoner

Indiana University Press

Bloomington & London

Manufactured in the United States of America

Library of Congress Cataloging in Publication Data
Wagoner, David.
    Who shall be the sun?

    1. Indians of North America—Northwest coast
of North America—Poetry. 2. Indians of North
America—Northwest, Pacific—Poetry. I. Title
PS3545.A345W49   811'.5'4   78–1836
ISBN 0–253–36527–9
    2   3   4   5   82   81   80   79

In memory of Franz Boas (1858–1942)
and to Na–To–Wa–Ki with love

Contents

5. The Songs of Only-One

6. Northwest Coast Indian Myths and Legends

7. The Songs of He-Catches-Nothing

Acknowledgments

The twenty-seven poems reprinted from *Collected Poems, 1956–1976*, appeared originally in *The New Yorker, Virginia Quarterly Review, Poetry, The Hudson Review, Poetry Now,* and *The American Poetry Review.*

The fifty-one new poems appeared in the following periodicals in the years shown: "Only One," "Song While Dancing Around an Empty Village," "Song of Under-the-Fire-Woman," "Song for the Renewal of Power," "Song for the Fishing of the Dead," "Song for the Coming of Smallpox," "Song for the Raising of a Medicine Pole," "The Dance of Only-One and Dead Man," "Song from the Land of the Dead" in *Chicago Review* (1977); "Loon," "Snow Goose and Southwind's Daughter," "How Southeast Came to the Dancing House" in *Loon* (1977); "Fireweed" in *Fireweed* (1977); "How Coyote Learned the Five Songs of Water" in *The Chowder Review* (1977); "Devil's Club" in *Blue Unicorn* (1977); "The Boy Who Became Seagull" in *Times Literary Supplement* (1977); "Touched-by-the-Moon" in *Iowa Review* (1977); "The Man Who Ate Himself" in *Kayak* (1978); "How Young Fox and Young Coyote Went Hungry," "How Coyote Became Young Coyote" in *Prairie Schooner* (1978); "Wild Man," "Woman-Asleep," "How Fish-Catcher Lost His Salmon," "Blindman," "Cloud-Watcher," in *Northwest Review* (1978); "How Lies-in-the-Water Became Seaweed" in *Virginia Quarterly Review* (1978); "The Burial of Salmon-Flying" in *Salmagundi* (1978); "Wood-Carver and Cedar-Woman" in *Ohio Review* (1978); "Sun Dog" in *Review La Booche* (1978); "Burial Song" in *Poetry* (1978); "Salmon Boy," "The Boy Who Became Sky," "How Canoe-Maker Fought with Southeast," "How Raven Came to the Feast" in *Antaeus* (1978); "How Raven Stole Light" in *Seattle Review* (1978); "The Man Who Killed Too Many," "How Owl Stole Back His Father," "How Raven Stole Beaver's Pond" in *Seneca Review* (1978); "How She-Cannot-Speak Ran Away," "Star-Woman-Falling," "Moon-Skin" in *Chariton Review* (1978); "He-Catches-Nothing," "Song Asking for Mercy from the Bushes," "Song After Fasting in a Tree," "Song from the Roof of a Flooded Lodge," "Song After Being Abandoned," "Song for the Death of Hummingbird," "Song from the Lodge of the Shadow People," "Song of a Man Who Rushed at the Enemy" in *Poetry Now* (1978).

Author's Note

These are not translations, though the narratives in sections 4 and 6 might be called retellings and owe their existence to the storytellers of the Kutenai, Nez Perce, Coeur d'Alene, Lillooet, Cathlamet, Coos, Chinook, Nootka, Kwakiutl, Haida, Tsimshian, and Tlingit tribes.

Those who may know only one version of some of these narratives may find unexpected details or turns of events in them, but, for example, the plot of the poem I have called "Star-Woman-Falling" occurs in at least nineteen versions among nineteen different tribes, and the same is true of many of the others. I often had to choose among garbled or transposed details from literal translations of several storytellers (some of whom were more gifted at the art than others), to condense and reconstruct, but I don't think I need to apologize, any more than Indian storytellers would have then or would now. Their fondness for borrowing and embellishing is everywhere evident in a cross-check of the work of pioneer turn-of-the-century anthropologists such as Franz Boas and John R. Swanton.

The poems in section 1 and the poems that I have called songs are less directly in the debt of Plateau and Northwest Coast Indian mythology, but would have been impossible for me to write without my having heard and read the songs and stories and read about and directly experienced the ways of American Indians.

Despite some of their less admirable characteristics historically—the glorification of warfare, the taking of slaves, the rigidity of some of their social structures, which are all too familiar as "human" failings among white men—the American Indians maintained at least one spiritual trait (essentially animistic) that I find particularly admirable and worthy of imitation, one that makes the frequently mocked eighteenth-century phrase *Noble Savage* worth thoughtful reexamination: they did not place themselves above their organic and inorganic companions on earth but recognized with awe that they shared the planet as equals with animals, fish, birds, trees, rivers, bushes, stones, and such phenomena as weather and natural disasters. This attitude made them more alert, humbler, and, I suspect, wiser than those whom the more northerly coastal tribes called "The Iron People" and the more southerly tribes called "The Moving People," two names that still fit white men uncomfortably well.

Who Shall Be the Sun?

1. Initiation

Searching in the Britannia Tavern

(TO EARL LUND, CLALLAM TRIBE)

To get to the Land of the Dead, you must go through
The place where everything is flying, past falling water
To the curb, across the sidewalk, stumbling, to the hunting ground.
Sleeping by day and moving only by night, you will come
To the place where you must sink, then rise, then enter
The abrupt silence where they have hidden your soul.

Having no one to be, the Dead steal souls. They lie
In wait in the middle of the floor, or spraddle for balance,
Their eyes burnt out. Those climbing toward the door
Have never entered. Those descending never arrive. They stand
Facing in different directions, blinking at walls, remembering
Nothing about your life. Remember, you told me:

Only a spirit can grapple with the Dead.
It must be danced or it never appears. You must watch for it
At night, or walk all day in your sleep, or stay under water
To make it come to you. When it enters, nothing stands still.
The wall is the floor, the floor and ceiling are walls,
Its voice is breaking in your ears, its broken speech
Is saying what you must know, the Dead are falling
Against each other, rattling their helpless fingers, remember,
The First People changed into bears, into rocks and fish,
Into trees, beavers, and birds, when they learned that men were
        coming,
And there, stalking toward you, the dark one is Tah-mah-no-us,
One Who Has Never Changed, his terrible mouth is smiling, he
        bears
Your soul slowly toward you in cupped hands.

3

Old Man, Old Man

Young men, not knowing what to remember,
Come to this hiding place of the moons and years,
To this Old Man. Old Man, they say, where should we go?
Where did you find what you remember? Was it perched in a tree?
Did it hover deep in the white water? Was it covered over
With dead stalks in the grass? Will we taste it
If our mouths have long lain empty?
Will we feel it between our eyes if we face the wind
All night, and turn the color of earth?
If we lie down in the rain, can we remember sunlight?

He answers, I have become the best and worst I dreamed.
When I move my feet, the ground moves under them.
When I lie down, I fit the earth too well.
Stones long under water will burst in the fire, but stones
Long in the sun and under the dry night
Will ring when you strike them. Or break in two.
There were always many places to beg for answers:
Now the places themselves have come in close to be told.
I have called even my voice in close to whisper with it:
Every secret is as near as your fingers.
If your heart stutters with pain and hope,
Bend forward over it like a man at a small campfire.

Lost

Stand still. The trees ahead and bushes beside you
Are not lost. Wherever you are is called Here,
And you must treat it as a powerful stranger,
Must ask permission to know it and be known.
The forest breathes. Listen. It answers,
I have made this place around you.
If you leave it, you may come back again, saying Here.
No two trees are the same to Raven.
No two branches are the same to Wren.
If what a tree or a bush does is lost on you,
You are surely lost. Stand still. The forest knows
Where you are. You must let it find you.

Fog

Though your brothers, after the long hunt and the fasting,
After holding still, have found Fox, Bear Mother,
Or Snake at their sides and taken them
Into the empty mouths of their spirits,
Do not be jealous. They will be cunning
Or strong or good at dreaming. Do not be ashamed
That you—when the day changed, when the first hour
Came falling suddenly over the last hour—
Found only Fog as the eye of your heart opened.

Now when your feet touch earth, nothing will know you.
You will move without moving a leaf,
Climb the steep cliffside as easily as Hawk,
Cross water, pass silently as Owl.
You will become trees by holding them inside you,
And tall stones, become a whole valley
Where birds fall still, where men stay close to fires.
You without wings or hands will gleam against them,
They will breathe you, they will be lost in you,
Your song will be the silence between their songs,
Your white darkness will teach them,
You will wrap all love and fear in a beautiful blindness.

2. Seven Songs for an Old Voice

Fire Song

I watch the point of the twirling stick
Where you are sleeping, where you will come again.
Already your breath, pale as fog through a vine-maple,
Is rising through shreds of cedarbark toward me.
Open your dark-red eye, Fire-brother.
Here is my breath to warm you. You may have all my breath.
Show me your yellow tongue, and I will feed you
Alder and black locust in thick branches
To gnaw in half like Beaver. Now, with you beside me,
I can see the eyes of the First People staring toward us
Hungrily, with the hollow look of Soul-Stealers.
Hold them out at the thin edge of darkness, and I will keep you
As long and as well as I keep myself through the night.
Toward dawn, you may lie down slowly, drift slowly out of the
      ashes
To sleep again at the cold point of my spirit.

Song for the Maker of Nightmares

You start your campfire on my breast like a mad grandfather
And eat my sleep for your food. Whenever you waken,
I must redden for war with her grunting children's children—
Thorn Cheek, Skinless Foot, Old Knife at the Lips, Moss Face,
Mouth-changer No One Hears, Lost Hand, my terrible brothers.
If you fall asleep in the middle of my fear, I come back
To claim my throat and my numb belly, like a dog
Who has strayed too far at night and swallowed his voice
At the first yawning of Bear Mother. Tonight I have no charms
To make you sleep. Begin again. Call out of their burrows like
    woodworms
Stump, Mouse Woman, Snag, Split Man. Even in my terror
I must believe you: I will drink what you bring me in my broken
    skull,
The bitter water which once was sweet as morning.

Song for the Soul Going Away

I have wakened and found you gone
On a day torn loose from its moon, uprooted
And wilting. How can I call you back with dust in my mouth?
My words lie dead on the ground like leaves. Night speech,
Water speech, the speech of rushes and brambles
Have thinned to muttering and a vague crackle,
And the bird in my ribcage has turned black and silent.
Where a man would stand, I sit. Where a man would sit,
I lie down burning. Where a man would speak,
My voice shrinks backward into its dark hovel.
Dragonfly has taken his glitter from the pool,
Birds' eggs are stones, all berries wither.
Without you, my eyes make nothing of light and shadow,
And the cup of each eyelid has run dry.
I go as aimless as my feet among sticks and stones,
Thinking of you on your mad, bodiless journey.

Dark Song

The faint scraping of stalk against leaf, the twig
And the caught thorn not quite breaking, yielding
Slowly in the night, are nothing
To fear: nothing knows
I am in this darkness, nothing knows which way
My dangerous eyes are turned. When young,
I bit the dark and clawed it, held my knife under its deep belly,
Set fire to it, jabbed it with sticks, strutted unseeing
Through its heart to my own rescue.
Now what stands behind my back is afraid:
I wait for longer than it can wait,
Listening, moving less than shadows.
It is mine now, soft as the breath of Owl.

Song for the Soul Returning

Without singing, without the binding of midnight,
Without leaping or rattling, you have come back
To lodge yourself in the deep fibres under my heart,
More closely woven than a salmonberry thicket.
I had struck the rocks in your name, but no one answered.
Left empty under the broken wings of Sun,
I had tasted and learned nothing. Now the creek no longer
Falters from stone to stone with a dead fishtailing
But bursts like the ledges of dawn, East Wind and West Wind
Meet on the hillside, and the softening earth
Spreads wide for my feet where they have never dared to go.
Out of the silent holts of willow and hazel, the wild horses,
Ears forward, come toward us, hearing your voice rise from my
        mouth.
My hands, whose craft had disappeared, search out each other
To shelter the warm world returning between them.

Song for the First People

When you learned that men were coming, you changed into rocks,
Into fish and birds, into flowers and rivers in despair of us.
The tree under which I bend may be you,
That stone by the fire, Nighthawk swooping
And crying out over the swamp reeds, the reeds themselves.
Have I held you too lightly all my mornings?
I have broken your silence, dipped you up
Carelessly in my hands and drunk you, burnt you,
Carved you, slit your calm throat and danced on your skin,
Made charms of your bones. You have endured
All of it, suffering my foolishness
As the old wait quietly among clumsy children.
Now others are coming, neither like you nor like men.
I must change, First People. How do I change myself?
If no one can teach me the long will of Cedar,
Let me become Water Dog, Bitterroot, or Shut Beak.
Change me. Forgive me. I will learn to crawl, stand, or fly
Anywhere among you, forever, as though among great elders.

Death Song

I touch the earth on all fours like a child,
And now my forehead touches the earth.
For the sake of my joys, Sleepmaker, let me in.
I have turned away from none of the six directions.
I have praised the rising and the dying wind,
Water falling or vanishing, even the end of grass.
I have welcomed the seasons equally
And been one with all weather from the wild to the silent.
The only blood left on my hands is my own: now my heart
Will be strict, admitting none, letting none go.
Close all my mouths. I will sleep inside of sleep,
Honoring the gift of darkness till it breaks.
I sing for a cold beginning.

3. Songs for the Dream-Catchers

Song for the Painting of the Dead

Now, in the black branches
Perched stiff or hanging
With your voices broken,
You have come back, Dead Ones.

Sit crooked at the fire
While I gather the hard knot
Of my heart, as hard as yours,
While I gather the blood of flowers,

The sweat of Sky and Sun.
Here, with my shaking fingers
I will touch your faces.
I will fill your lost eyes.

Again, you will paint for war.
I will paint the bare bones
With skin as tight as drumskin,
With the loud strokes of Breathmaker.

You will move and sing.
None will go who does not return.
None will be here, Dead Ones,
Who has not been yours.

Song for the Eating of Barnacles

I carry the stones you cling to
And heap them ashore.
Sharp, white-clustered Barnacles,
Teeth of Salt Woman, forgive me:
I must make you a flat house
Out of sticks and eel grass
And set it on fire.

Now over the mud-flats
I call the chalky smoke
To loosen your chalk roots.
You must fall out of the tide's jaw
To sleep in my basket,
Then dream of the feast
Where I will taste your secret.

Do not be afraid: my teeth
Will close against your teeth,
Pale and hard as yours.
I do what you have done
In the swelling and shrinking water,
What you will do again when I throw you
Back to gray Sea Mother.

Song against the Sky

What is wrong with Sky?
Look, he is crumbling fire
Over the white river.
He is spilling all the stars
Out of the horn spoon
To hiss in the ocean.
He is shattering, shattering
The ice of his heart
And flinging the pieces here
To splinter the last alder.
He has cut the moon
In half, and again in half
To be skinned and eaten.
We must make war
Against this cracking Sky
Soon or be broken:
He has broken the post of heaven.

Song for a Stolen Soul

Sky, I am standing
Beneath your bitter morning,
Holding my song
Shut like a hawk's wing.

Sky, you know
I can fly above you.
I can split the skull of Rainbow,
Scatter the ashes of snow.

You know Four Winds would come
Now if I called them,
Even the Second Moon
If I spoke its true name.

I will not wait for darkness
Again to climb to your house.
Here in your blue face
The wing of my song stretches.

Sky, now you will break
At the first swift stroke
Of my song's beak.
Give my soul back!

Song for the Skull of Black Bear

You came out of pity for my empty mouth
And the wind over my shoulders
As heavy as your paws.
We stood against each other
In the Dance of the Torn Bellies,
But your robe, even without you,
Was heavier than I could carry.
Hung from my neck, your claws
Have shamed my fingers.

Once I was a true hunter
Afraid to speak your name—
Blue Tongue, Old Crooked Foot,
Wearer of the mask Many Bees,
Tree Carver, Honey Snout,
Stands-Like-a-Man, Snow Sleeper
With breath the color of ghosts.
Now I must join you. Now I say
Black Bear, Black Bear.

I have blackened my face
To be your skin, to honor
The thin blood I must give you.
Like your skull in the thick woods
You will hide in the thick of my sleep.
I will dream you and your jaws.
In the Moon of Half-ripeness
You will redden your face to mourn me
When my skull lies by yours.

Song for the Bones of Salmon

I have counted your bones,
Salmon, my sister,
Even the thin gillbones
Like the nets of Spider.
Only a few are broken.
Let this song be those bones.

Let it be the scales lost
On the hard stones
Where you strained at nesting.
Let my song be your cupped eye
Where the flies have come for days
As if to the last spring.

Let it be your flesh,
The long muscles stronger
Than the white water.
Let my song fill your mouth
Like your own strange breath,
The wind inside the river.

Now go downstream swiftly,
Your mouth to its mouth.
Take my song into the salt.
Feed long, feed for us both,
And I will wait gladly
Till you come again to die.

Song for Ice

Ice, I ask for nothing
From the nine spirits
Between Ice-Dying
And Ice-Being-Born:
If you wish to crack
As deep as Earthmaker,
Or burst into rainbows
Under my slit eyes
Peering through whalebone,
Or heave in slabs,
Or bulge into clouds
Harder than ax-heads,
Or turn to a crooked sky
Where Snow Goose and Bear
Can neither swim nor stand,
Or be Ice-Clear, Ice-Hollow,
Ice-White-With-Anger,
Or Ice-Groaning-With-Hunger,
You will do as you please.

If you drift in the night,
Turning your floes around
Under my dreaming feet
Till every step takes back
A step of my journey,
I will not sing against you.
Ice, we must bear each other.
Have we not frozen together
In the long darkness

And stretched in the same weather
As hard and cold as brothers?
Will we not shrink, then turn
To the same wild water?

4. Plateau Indian Myths and Legends

Who Shall Be the Sun?

The People said, "Who shall be the sun?"
Raven cried, "Raven! Raven!"
He imagined rising and setting
Grandly, his great wings spreading over the People.
All days would belong to him. No one
Would see the earth without marvelous Raven.

He rose then out of the thick night.
He crooked his ragged wings, flapping them wildly,
Yet he made evening all day long,
Nothing but gloom in the woods, shade on the rivers.
The People grunted: "Get away from the sky!
You are too dark! Come down, foolish Raven!"

The People said, "Someone else must try."
Hawk screamed, "Hawk! Hawk!"
He imagined rising and rising
High over the specks of the tiny People.
He would be alone, taller than the wind. No one
Would cast a shadow without brilliant Hawk.

He rose then out of the empty night.
He soared and climbed into the yellow air
As high as noon, clenching his talons,
His bright wings flashing in the eye of the heavens.
The People squinted and shouted: "Too much daylight!
Get out of the sky! Come down, ignorant Hawk!"

The People Said, "But we must have someone."
Coyote howled, "Coyote! Coyote!"
He imagined jumping and running
Low over the bent heads of the People.
He would make them crouch all day. No one
Would escape the tricks of clever Coyote.

He rose then out of the hole of night.
He darted and leaped over the red clouds
As swift as stormfire, his jaws gleaming,
His wild breath burning over the crowns of trees.
The People sweated and sputtered, diving into water,
"You will cook the earth! Come down, crazy Coyote!"

The People said, "We shall have no sun at all!"
But Snake whispered, "I have dreamed I was the sun."
Raven, Hawk, and Coyote mocked him by torchlight:
"You cannot scream or howl! You cannot run or fly!
You cannot burn, dazzle, or blacken the earth!
How can you be the sun!" "By dreaming," Snake whispered.

He rose then out of the rich night.
He coiled in a ball, low in the sky.
Slowly he shed the Red Skin of Dawn,
The Skin of the Blue Noontime, the Skin of Gold,
And last the Skin of Darkness, and the People
Slept in their lodges, safe, till he coiled again.

How Coyote Became Rock's Brother

Coyote walked far, lost in the heat of the day.
Sweating, he sat on Rock and said, "My brother,
You may have my robe." He threw it aside
Over Rock's heavy shoulders and wandered on.

A great cloud blackened the earth. Coyote turned
And hurried back to Rock sitting still and dry.
Coyote said, "Give me my robe against the rain."
Rock whispered through the robe, "Now it is mine."

"You have no need of a robe," Coyote said and snatched it
And wrapped it around him, walking into the storm.
But soon, behind, he heard something like thunder
And saw Rock rumbling after him: "Give me my robe!"

Coyote ran past Nighthawk, crying, "Help me! Help me!
Rock is chasing us all!" But Nighthawk said, "No.
Rock is my nest. All night I ride on the wind,
All day I sleep on Rock: he is my day-cloud."

Coyote ran past Buffalo, crying, "Save me! Save me!
Rock wants to kill us all!" But Buffalo
Said, "No. When the People hunt me, Rock deceives them:
We look the same. He splits their strongest arrows."

Coyote ran past Bear, crying, "Only you can help me!
Rock wants to crush us all!" But Bear said, "No.
Rock is the roof of my lodge. He lasts through the Moon
Of the Cracking Trees. He is my winter sky."

Coyote stood alone in the rain then, and Rock tumbled
Closer and closer, bumping and booming.
He was no day-cloud. He was no good protector
Against the shafts of the hunting weather.

Kneeling, Coyote offered his robe again, and Rock
Halted against his forehead, solid and cold.
"I need no robe," Rock said. "I wear this rain.
Tomorrow I wear the sun or the snow, no matter."

Coyote opened his arms and clung to Rock. Rock said,
"I hear your heart. Now you may stand against me.
No one will hunt you. You may sleep beneath me
With or without a robe. Welcome, lost brother."

How Coyote Stole Rain

It had not rained since the Moon of Bitterroot.
The river died. The People had no water.
Coyote said, "I will go to the lodge of Rain-Keeper."

He gathered Louse, Wood-tick, and Flea. He ran
Down the dry riverbed to its empty mouth
And found a lodge like a cloud with a shut door.

While Coyote hid, Louse, Wood-tick, and Flea
Crawled through the floor to find Rain-Keeper's daughter.
They drank with her. They danced with her in the night.

She woke in their arms and broke the lodge door, weeping,
And Coyote caught her and ran back to the mountains.
Rain-Keeper followed, rumbling upstream and storming.

Coyote shouted, "The door of Rain-Keeper's lodge
Must open to let us have the tears of his daughter!"
And the People drank and danced by the full river.

Why Coyote Howls Only at Night

Coyote had three sons. He left them playing
Alone in his safe tipi while he went hunting.
But they crawled into the sunlight, and that Sun
Drank from their small mouths all day and killed them.

Coyote howled at Moon. Moon listened and wept.
At dawn Coyote hid where Sky first opens,
Waited and leaped straight at Sun's burning breast
And tore it open, tore out the huge heart.

Sun died, the air turned black, the rivers froze.
Coyote dragged that heart, stumbling and falling,
Over the frozen prairie, singing his anger.
But the People said, "You will kill us, crazy Coyote!"

Tasting that heart, Coyote dragged it back
Where Sun stood still in the darkness. He thrust it
Into the empty breast. Sun rose again,
The rivers melted, and the People lived.

But Coyote remembered. He sings only to Moon.

How Young Fox and Young Coyote Went Hungry

Coyote and Fox had sons. One night in their tipi
Young Coyote said, "Father, what is my power?"
Coyote said, "Moonlight-Touching-the-Ground."
Young Fox said, "Father, what is my power?"
Fox said, "Darkness-of-Night." Tying those powers
Slyly behind them, the two sons went out hunting.

They crept into the village to steal meat,
And Young Coyote said, "If the People see us,
They will find only red and silver shadows
Beyond their campfire. If the People chase us,
We will untie Moonlight-Touching-the-Ground
And Darkness-of-Night. No one can catch us."

But Young Fox said, "I have never used my power."
And Young Coyote shouted, "It is like playing!"
The People saw their red and silver shadows
Crossing the grass. Young Coyote began laughing.
He tried to untie Moonlight-Touching-the-Ground,
But he was laughing, and the People caught him.

Now it was not a game. They bound him with rawhide
And cut off all his soft long silver hair.
The People were poking and laughing. He began howling,
And Young Fox heard him deep in his Night-Bush
And came again, creeping, bringing his darkness.
While the People slept, Young Fox bit through that rawhide.

And Young Coyote was running, running so fast
When he untied Moonlight-Touching-the-Ground
He was not touching the ground. He left no tracks
For the People to follow, only a light hoarfrost
Over the grass-crowns. He and Young Fox ran hungry,
Moon-Bush with Night-Bush, back to their fathers' tipi.

How Coyote Became Young Coyote

Coyote was old. Out hunting, Young Coyote
Would tell him, "Stay here! Crawl there! Make fire! "
Coyote sat here, crawled there, but in his heart
He made a fire that burned him like pitch-wood.

Squirrel sat in a tree, and Young Coyote
Took off his fur and, naked, clawed the bark
And climbed and crawled through branches after Squirrel.
Coyote stayed below, singing for power.

And the tree groaned and grew, stretching its limbs
Out of its slow dream. Young Coyote climbed,
But the tree grew faster. He followed, and Squirrel
Made a hole in the sky and disappeared.

Coyote put on the skin of his son and ran
To Young Coyote's wives, White Swan and Cricket.
He cried, "My father is dead! " And White Swan soothed him,
But Cricket scuttled away under the grass.

White Swan was beautiful. She pecked Coyote,
Preened his young fur, and petted him into laughing.
Cricket was ugly. When she heard that laughter,
She left the village, mourning her lost husband.

Above the sky in the gray fields, Young Coyote,
Naked and hungry, crawled on the bare ground.
He ran, he sat, found nothing, made no fire,
And dreamed of the fur no longer around him.

The Spider People came, and he said, "Grandfathers,
I am dying." They hissed and fed him the blood of Moth.
They spun a thread, wound it around his body,
And let him down to earth in the morning.

Cricket was weeping under stones. He heard her
There in her death-lodge, and he called to her,
And Cricket came to his naked arms and knew him.
They went back to the village, weeping and laughing.

Young Coyote said, "My father, give me my fur."
While White Swan flew away, crying and wild,
Coyote struggled out of that young skin,
Grown old and stiff, hunching close to the fire.

How Coyote Learned the Five Songs of Water

When he heard that song, Coyote was sleeping.
It was Water dripping on stone. He listened
As he lay on the dry creekbed. It kept dripping
Till it filled his head, and he went to find it.
He said, "That song is over! Be quiet!"

But Water dripped on stone, so Coyote licked it.
He said, "I will sing that song myself if I want it."
But Water went on dripping, so Coyote drank it,
Saying, "Sing a new song in my belly!" But that Water
Kept dripping and dripping. Coyote kicked it.

He moved down slope in the dust, stiff-legged, sleepy.
Now he was thirsty. He had never felt so thirsty.
When he lay down, that song was in his head
Still dripping and dripping on the stone of his tongue.
Then he heard Water running after him.

It trickled toward him, and he licked it all,
Saying "Water, you are singing a good song!"
Now it flowed up his chest. He tried to drink it,
Choking and saying, "Three songs are too many!"
But it came pouring its fourth song, brown and angry.

Coyote drank his belly full, filled his whole heart,
His throat, his eyes. Oh, he was drinking
Deeper than he was tall. He was hearing Water
Singing inside out. In his ears that Water was singing
Its last song for the drowning of Coyote.

Touched-by-the-Moon

That woman had given her heart to Crow-catcher.
She said, "Who is beautiful?" He said, "Crow's Egg."
Strand by strand she pulled out her long hair.

She said, "Who is beautiful?" He said, "Stone-Wearing-Snow."
And she plucked out her eyebrows and eyelashes
Till her face and her scalp seemed worn by weather.

She said, "Who is beautiful?" He said, "Ice-on-the-Mountain."
She pulled out every hair on her body
And lay as smooth as water without wind.

She said, "Who is beautiful?" And he said, "Moon,"
Looking away, turning away, going away.
So she walked out by moonlight to die.

But the Spider People lifted her up to Moon,
And Moon touched her and said, "Crow's Egg, Stone-Wearing-
      Snow,
And Ice-on-the-Mountain are your sisters."

All of her hair grew back more sleek, more shiny.
Her skin was like Moon's. Slowly the Spider People
Let her down from their web into the morning.

Crow-catcher saw her. Now she was beautiful,
And he went toward her. But Touched-by-the-Moon
Wandered away to live with her sisters,

Crow's Egg who says, *Young darkness waiting*,
Stone-Wearing-Snow who says, *I will not melt*,
Ice-on-the-Mountain who says, *Here it is coldest*.

40

How Owl Won Back His Father

No one had seen Owl's father since the Moon
Of Snow-Melting. The People were afraid
Ghosts had taken him over the Black River
Or Flint-Eater held him in Cave of the Crooked Wind.

Owl went hunting at night, and he caught Mouse.
Mouse said, "You will spit my bones. If you spare me,
I will take you to your father." So Owl went with him
Far toward the sea to the lodge of Mouse Woman.

Mouse Woman said, "He gambled his arms and legs,
His body, his hair and eyes, by shooting arrows
Against Sturgeon." Owl saw the eyeless, hairless
Head of his father swinging in her smoke-hole.

Bluejay cried, "My great chief Sturgeon has heard
Young Owl is ready to gamble. Bring your bow.
Your father's arms and legs for yours, his body,
His hair, and eyes for yours," and Owl said, "Yes."

He fledged his arrows with his own dark feathers.
He flaked his arrowheads from obsidian
And strung his bow with sinew of Black Elk
And went down to the shore where Sturgeon waited.

His belly swelled and shrank like Noise-of-the Surf.
His mouth was chewing and grunting. Noise-of-the-Surf
Was chewing and grunting, and Sturgeon flashed his belly,
Blazing, shining, straight into Owl's eyes.

Mouse Woman whispered, "Your father could not wait.
He missed with all his arrows." So Owl stood waiting,
His eyes full of that flashing, while Grandmother Sun
Crept down the sky to touch the mat of the sea.

Sturgeon shouted, "Let Owl go back to his lodge
And sleep all day and hunt for mice in the night! "
But Owl kept waiting. Noise-of-the-Surf grew louder,
Came chewing closer, and Sturgeon glittered his belly.

When Grandmother Sun folded her blanket, Owl
Shot his first arrow and won his father's arms,
Again, his legs and body, again and again,
His hair and his eyes, all growing back together.

Owl covered Sturgeon's belly with green mud,
Stuck flint against his back, and flung him far
Into the grunting mouth of Noise-of-the-Surf,
Then led his father home through the good darkness.

Snow Goose and Southwind's Daughter

Snow Goose flew far and far to the lodge of Northwind
And, weak and hungry, sat by the dead fire
Where Northwind's daughter said, "I will feed you."

Northwind was angry. The blue stones of his eyes
Darkened, his fingers crackled like frozen roots
While he shifted and turned under his gray blankets.

Northwind's cold daughter said, "Here is your bowl."
She was as white as Snow Goose, but thin and hard.
Her eyes were slits in bone, her hair gray moss.

Cracking his ice-blue lips till they split open,
Northwind took that food and emptied the bowl.
Snow Goose flew hungry to the lodge of Southwind.

He sat by the good fire, silent and shaking.
Southwind's warm daughter said, "I will feed you."
Her eyes were soft, her hair was like wild wheat.

Snow Goose ate from the bowl till his breast and belly
Grew round and sleek. He sang, "Here is my wife!"
And her father nodded slowly among red blankets.

Northwind turned black with anger. He armed himself
With spears of ice and stormed into the south,
Flinging gray stones and blankets over that lodge.

But Southwind painted for war, and the spears melted,
Those stones and blankets melted north through the forest,
And Snow Goose bent his neck to Southwind's daughter.

Star-Woman-Falling

She was too frightened to be married. She hid
When those young men walked by, standing and glancing,
Being tall for her, showing their straight bodies,
Their hair shining, their feathers sleek in the sunlight.
They opened their blankets, but she ran away.

She lay down in a field under many stars:
Blue Star, Red Star, Star-Making-Rainbows,
Horn Star, Arrow Star, Star-Crossing-and-Burning.
Out of them all, she fixed on one pale star
And said, "I will marry that one. That is my husband."

She slept. She woke, afraid, in a strange village.
An old man sat beside her. He said, "My wife,
Now you are Star-Woman, married to Star-Falling.
You may go and gather roots with the others,
But stay away from trees." He fell asleep.

He was dry and crooked, his skin was cracked, his feet
Seemed stuck in the earth, his arms looked weak and stiff.
She saw young trees there, growing like young men,
Supple and limber, sleek leaves waving like feathers,
And women moved among them, digging and singing.

Star-Woman wept. She had married an old man
When these young men like trees stood all around her!
She went to Sprucetree and dug his roots with a stick,
Scratched hard at the ground and wept over her husband,
But jabbed too deep and made a hole in the sky.

She saw her village below, the People walking
Far underneath, the People singing and dancing.
She took a root of Sprucetree, long and thin,
The binder of strongest baskets. She held it
Tight in her hands and stepped down through the sky.

But the sheath of that root slipped off like a snakeskin,
And the People saw her become Star-Woman-Falling.

Sun Dog

That man was rich. He wore shell beads and copper,
Marten and Ermine. Wherever he walked
The People looked at him. They would try to please him.
They gave him many gifts, and he wore them
Or ate them or pushed them away, frowning.

Each dawn, he would lie in wait for the sunrise,
Would stare at the place where the sky opens.
If stormclouds hid it, he stormed at them,
But dawns without clouds, he would stare, then squint
At that bright Sun. He said, "I must go there."

The People said, "That is too far!" But he started,
Crossed rivers and lakes, climbed hills and rocks,
Made steps in snow, in ice, clung fast to clouds,
Bent Rainbow upright as a tree and climbed it,
Cut a hole in the sky, squeezing himself through.

Each morning, he saw that Sun grow brighter, more huge.
Each night, he dreamed of holding it in his arms,
More beautiful than a wife, richer and greater
Than the People or himself. He felt full of himself.
He would take that Sun and give it new children.

He came to a dark lodge on a mountain ridge.
No one was there, but it was filled with arrows,
Quivers and seashells, skins of Mountain Goat
And Buffalo, painted shields, stone axes,
All hanging from the burnt walls and the ceiling.

A bent old woman with a folded blanket
Stooped through the door and sat down at the fire,
Looking at him. She said, "Your eyes have followed
Me, morning by morning. I see you, Sun Dog.
You have come far. Now you may choose your power."

He glanced from arrows to axes, from skins to shells,
But from that woman's blanket, between folds,
He saw a glimmer like a burning knife
Sharper than his eyes. He said, "Grandmother Sun,
I will take my power by wearing your blanket."

She shook her head. "No one else may wear it."
He took it from her. "Grandmother, you are old.
Sit by the fire and sleep for many days."
She stared, her face the color of ashes, saying
Nothing. Sun Dog climbed back down to his village.

He unfolded that blanket there and threw it
Over his shoulders, burning bright as noon.
He wore Sun Blanket, walked slowly, brilliantly
For all the People to see, but he burned them.
They shrank from him and shrivelled, turning black.

He tore at that blanket, but his hands were closed.
It stuck to his skin. The People were dying.
He tried to strip it in the fork of an ashtree,
But it kept burning around him. The blood of the People
Was drying in their veins, their lodges smoking.

He rolled in a thicket, scraped himself on rocks,
But Sun Blanket roared like the mouth of Fire-catcher.
He ran to the river. Water leaped into clouds
And flew to the north like Snow Geese carrying summer,
And the People turned to ashes, blown to the north.

Sun Dog knelt and wept. Now there was no one
To look at him, to give him food and gifts,
No one to watch him walking, sitting, or dreaming,
No one to hear him speaking. When Grandmother Sun
Peeled off her blanket, Sun Dog was burning.

The Man Who Ate Himself

He killed a bighorn sheep in the mountains.
He skinned it, cut it in strips for his drying-frame,
All but the head, then made his fire for the night
And cooked some meat, but it tasted like snow-melt.
Still hungry, he cooked more. It tasted like rock-dust.
Cooked more, all of it. It tasted like East Wind.
The head of Bighorn Sheep said, *Eat your own body*.

That hunter cut a strip from his breast and cooked it,
And it tasted like the breast of his mother.
He cooked a piece of his tongue and ate it,
And it tasted like the tongue of his wife.
He ate a piece of his heart, he ate his eyes,
They tasted like the eyes and heart of his daughter.
Then he ate all his brains in a wild feast.

Now he was only bones with a throat and belly.
Now he was Bones-Walking. His belly was filled
With snow-melt, rock-dust, East Wind, and himself,
But he was still hungry. He fastened the horns
Of Bighorn Sheep to his empty forehead
And came down from the mountains to his village
To eat his mother, his wife, and his daughter.

His daughter was sleeping. Sandhill Crane was flying
And calling, *Your father is Bones-Walking.*
He wants to eat you. She hurried to tell her mother,
Her mother hurried to tell her husband's mother,
And when Bones-Walking rattled into the village,
The People ran. Rain, dust, and wind came with him.
His horns were shaking, and he screamed, "I love you!"

His mother said, "Where are you? Where have you gone?
We love you!" His wife reached out to hold him,
But he ate them both, hugging them in his belly.
Now they were his. Now they would stay with him
Like his own eaten heart and his eaten eyes.
He made a fire, ready to cook his daughter,
To linger over every part of her body.

But Sandhill Crane was calling to her again:
*You must dance for him on the steepest riverbank
By the deepest water.* With her wings spread wide,
Sandhill Crane went dancing, and that daughter
Danced on the loose clay with her arms floating,
And Bones-Walking came lurching after her,
Heavy and hungry, and fell and drowned in the river.

5. The Songs of Only-One

Only-One

That boy wanted to be more than a boy.
He gathered shells. They stayed hollow.
He rattled birdbones. No birds would grow on them.
His drumboard made a lost-in-the-wind sound,
And no one would dance to it. He danced alone.

He went down to the sea. There stood Heron
On one leg in the shallows, its beak broken,
Waiting to die alone. That boy reached out
And sharpened Heron's beak, and Heron stabbed him
Deep in one eye, saying, "Only-One!"

Now he saw only with his missing eye,
Saw Heron fly on one wing, half a moon
Crossing a half-sky ending in nothing,
Saw half-clouds split like thighbones, a half-sun
Spilling its redness shoreward on half-waves.

And a girl stood in the water on one leg,
Her long hair streaming down over one shoulder.
One eye was beautiful. The other was darkness.
She lifted one arm, but the other stayed in shadow.
Oh, he danced for her! He danced for her!

He rattled birdbones and shells in the half-light.
He struck the drumboard. He was not that boy
Dancing Alone. Half the earth danced with him.
The red half-sun gleamed on half his body,
And he sang her the first dream song of Only-One.

She came to him out of the broken sea,
And they went side by side into the village.
The People smiled in their hands. His mother and father
Hid their fingers. He said, "This is my bride
Called Stands-on-the-Shore. I am not alone."

But the People said, "Where is this bride?"
His father said, "There is no one beside you."
His mother said, "There is only sea-mist."
The People said, "He was dancing by crazy water."
Stands-on-the-Shore turned half away and vanished.

Only-One ran to find her, tripped by half-stones
And stumbling among half-trees onto the sand.
There by the cracked-in-half moon he saw her standing
Again in the shallows, preening blue feathers.
When he called, she stretched one wing and flew toward him.

Song while Dancing around
an Empty Village

They are dead in my village.
I see them sleeping in lodges
Or lying on high death-posts
Or tied in trees as if fasting.

Killer Whale and Raven
Stand among them, broken.
Blackberry and salmonberry
Grow from their open mouths.

Sea Wolf, Beaver, Bear Mother
Have fallen against them.
The Crooked Beak of Heaven
Has nested in moss and lichen.

Now I untie the knot
Of my cold breath, to begin.
At my heels I wear the copper
Tail-feathers of Flicker.

Wherever I place my feet
They will make small fires.
I will make a fire-necklace
Burning like spirit copper

Around the neck of my village,
And the souls of the People
Will fill them again, will sing
In their empty bodies, dancing.

Song of Under-the-Fire-Woman

Sit still. Whatever you say
Or whisper I will hear
Under this hungry fire.
I will tell it to those who wear
Dream-catching copper
Around their necks forever:
Stone-Rib and Half-Man,
Clam's Eye and Cloud-Watcher,
Sky-Shining, Lover-of-Slaughter.
They wait in that other place
Where the black sun burns close.
They wait for food to burn
Here in my burning hair
So they may feast together.
Whatever you murmur
About them, I will remember.
I will tell Bent Finger,
Moldy Forehead, He-Travels-Behind-You,
Stone-Broken-Under-Stone.
Unless you blacken your lips
With my coals and be silent,
They will come back to claim
A share of your tongue.
Whisper, and I will burn it.

Song for the Fishing of the Dead

Downstream of the willows
This night the Dead are fishing
In the river. Their canoes,
Covered with moss, have holes
For eyes under the water.

They see the willow leaves,
Yellow, slender, float by,
And the Dead are catching them
In their nets, in the shadows
Of sprucetrees, as their Trout.

With their bone harpoons
There in the pools they spear
Dead branches as their Salmon.
If you sing, they fall silent.
If you whisper, they are gone.

Be still: they are singing
Like the river for the feast
In their longhouse, gathering stones
To burn in the dark fire there
As round as their lost moons.

Song for the Stealing of a Spring

This place where water grows
Out of stone, under willows,
Where the ax of Moon falls,
Cut-by-the-Halfmoon-Spring,
Come, the People are waiting.

They have thirsted for you.
I must gather you gently
In my robe for a night's journey.
Do not be afraid when Horned Owl
Shakes his mouse-rattle.

I will carry you, Spring-No-One-Has-Tasted.
I will plant you in this dry season
Where you will grow green and cold.
I, the dream-catcher Only-One,
I will do it, Rainbush, Rainskin.

Song for the Raising of a Medicine Pole

I wrestled the young pinetree,
Tall as three men, all day
Till it bowed and came with me,
Trailing its roots to my doorway,
And now I raise it and fasten it
Level, away from the earth,
And give it my dream shirt for a banner.

It will teach me to die wisely:
Its needles falling, its bark peeling
Slowly under the knife of the weather,
No longer bending or straining
Against the wind's wild shoulder,
But taking snowfall, rainfall, sunfall
As calmly as the fall of the sky.

It will say, *Under this wooden roof*
Lies a man who dreamed
But did not take that dream to war
Or on the red trail of the hunter.
Instead, he kept it here
To fight old Marrow-Eater
Who splits men's bones for dinner.

Song for the Renewal of Power

I have drunk seawater
To teach the salt
Again to my dry heart.

I, to whom Raven spoke
At the foot of the cradleboard
At the turn of low tide,

Who lost one eye
Sharpening the broken
Beak of Blue Heron,

I, the dream-catcher Only-One,
Must wait for my spirit
Where I first found it.

Goodbye, old brothers,
He-Sits-in-the-Woods,
He-Hurries-to-Sing.

For three days I must stand
Deep under the sea
With Starfoot-Walking.

Song for the Coming of Smallpox

At night sparks fly from them,
The ships of the Iron People.
Iron struck in the fire
Throws sparks, makes knives
And spearpoints harder than bone.

Wherever those sparks fall
They burn our smooth faces.
They burn, making holes
As deep as bone,
Setting fire to our bodies.

My spirit, when it first came,
Made a hole in my mind,
And I fell down, dreaming
What I must do and be
Through the long fire of my life.

The hole of my mouth
And the hole of my lost eye
Filled with new songs,
But the ships of the Iron People
Bring the mask of many holes.

Who wears it must fall down
With many holes in his mind,
Not iron in that fire,
Not stronger and harder,
But dreaming only of bones.

The Dance of Only-One and Dead Man

This night in the cold rain
Around us, I call you down
From your tall burial post
Where you have lain dreaming
The long dream of Cedar
Like that same seedling
Rooted deep in your dust.
I wrap your burial mat
As a dancing skirt around you.

Now we must dance, Dead Man.
The People are watching
In their lodges, their eyes closed,
Their feet remembering.
My rattle tells you to rise.
Like Nightwind, I blow across
The mouths of soft-wood whistles.
Who am I? says Dead Man.
I say, You are no one.

Dead Man says, *I know you.*
Why must I dance again
To the Singing of Only-One?
I say, The People must see you,
Even He-Chews-the-Days
Who eats only the air,
Even Under-the-Fire-Woman
Who tells secrets to spirits,
Even Moss, even Stone must see you.

Now you are dancing, Dead Man.
I have painted your breastbone
With the half-eaten Moon
Left to grow by Raven.
I have filled your skull
With my song made from seawater.
We shall dance together
Till the bloody hands of Morning
Tear Sky Blanket open.

Song from the Land of the Dead

Once I was Only-One. Now I am no one.
When I walk, I see only behind me.
No clouds pour forward out of the mouth of Sky
In a storm song. They are always going away.
Out of these shallow pools, the rain falls upward.
The only river flows uphill to its spring
And vanishes. The trees grow smaller.
They gather their dead leaves like a harvest
And sink into the unbroken earth.
I sit through noontime, once called *midnight*,
Wearing this empty body whose heart
No longer beats, whose blood stands still
As if listening. There is nothing to hear,
Nothing to hear me. I cannot hear
This voice I speak with.

Even this poor song ended
Before it began, slipped into my dry mouth
First with its silence, then with a cold music,
Then with a slowly dwindling speech,
Then a beginning, then its other silence.

6. Northwest Coast Indian Myths and Legends

Salmon Boy

That boy was hungry. His mother gave him Dog Salmon,
Only the head. It was not enough,
And he carried it hungry to the river's mouth
And fell down hungry. Salt water came from his eyes,
And he turned over and over. He turned into it.

And that boy was swimming under the water
With his round eyes open. He could not close them.
He was breathing the river through his mouth.
The river's mouth was in *his* mouth. He saw stones
Shimmering under him. Now he was Salmon Boy.

He saw the Salmon People waiting. They said, "This water
Is our wind. We are tired of swimming against the wind.
Come to the deep, calm valley of the sea.
We are hungry too. We must find the Herring People."
And they turned their green tails. Salmon Boy followed.

He saw Shell-Walking-Backwards, Woman-Who-Is-Half-Stone.
He heard the long, high howling of Wolf Whale,
Seal Woman's laughter, the whistling of Sea Snake,
Saw Loon Mother flying through branches of seaweed,
Felt Changer turn over far down in his sleep.

He followed to the edge of the sky where it opens
And closes, where Moon opens and closes forever,
And the Herring People brought feasts of eggs,
As many as stars, and Salmon Boy ate the stars
As if he flew among them, saying *Hungry, Hungry*.

But the Post of Heaven shook, and the rain fell
Like pieces of Moon, and the Salmon People swam,
Tasting sweet, saltless wind under the water,
Opening their mouths again to the river's mouth,
And Salmon Boy followed, full-bellied, not afraid.

He swam fastest of all. He leaped into the air
And smacked his blue-green silvery side, crying, *Eyo!
I jump!* again and again. Oh, he was Salmon Boy!
He could breathe everything! He could see everything!
He could eat everything! And then his father speared him.

He lay on the riverbank with his eyes open,
Saying nothing while his father emptied his belly.
He said nothing when his mother opened him wide
To dry in the sun. He was full of the sun.
All day he dried on sticks, staring upriver.

The Boy Who Became Sky

No man could have that woman, Mouth-of-the-River.
All were afraid of Fish-catcher, her stony father,
So she lay on the shore and gave herself to the sea,
And the sea gave her a boy in a broken shell.

Fish-catcher abandoned her. The People abandoned her.
But that boy grew, and she made him a copper bow
And copper arrows, and he hunted in the woods.
He hunted beside white water to feed her.

He brought her Cormorant and Goose,
Redwing, Bluejay, and Winter Wren.
She ate them all. But that boy kept all their skins
And all their feathers. He looked at them. He looked at them.

He said, "I am going to find my grandfather.
He must not leave you forever." His mother
Painted clouds on his forehead, and he walked far
From rock to bluff to creek through fog through rain.

At last he found the People. They were starving
By Inlet of Many Winds. "Grandfather Fish-catcher,
You must come back to my mother, Mouth-of-the-River,"
He said. "Look in my cloudy face and know it."

His grandfather said, "I have no daughter!"
That boy's face with stormclouds made him angry.
He said, "*My* grandson would be a fish-catcher!"
He climbed into a canoe, and that boy followed.

They left the shore, beaten by cross-waves
And blown by many winds. His grandfather sang,
Yeho yeholo! but the water would not be milk.
That boy cast out a bentwood-and-bone hook.

Oh, that boy put on the skin of Cormorant,
A blue throat gleaming against gleaming darkness.
He said, "Grandfather, say *Sky is shaking!*"
Fish-catcher felt afraid, but he said it.

That boy put on the skin of Goose, white above gray
With a black hood. "Grandfather, say *Sky
Is blowing away!*" Their canoe was blowing away
At the end of the island. Fish-catcher said it.

That boy put on the skin of Redwing, red
Over yellow, caught by the deepest blackness.
"Grandfather, say *Sky is returning!*" Fish-catcher
Said it, and the sea went flat and milky.

That boy put on the skin of Bluejay, blue
Spreading against blue, and said, "Grandfather,
Say *This is the lodge of Sky!*" When Fish-catcher said it,
The fishline sang the dream song of Halibut.

And up from the sea-bottom the great head came,
Trailing its nests of kelp, its eyes white stones,
And stared at them—old, huge Halibut Mother,
As wide as a river, and that boy let her go.

That boy put on the skin of Winter Wren,
Gold against earth-color, and he stood, he grew,
He said, "Grandfather, say *This is Sky!*" Fish-catcher
Said it and wept, saying, "Grandson! Grandson!"

That boy became Sky then, drifting away,
Wearing the skin of Wren like the skin of dawn
When the heavy, sleepy sons of Halibut Mother
Wait for the People under the calm water.

And the People went to find Mouth-of-the-River.

How Moss Grew Strong

Ice shouted, "My sons must be the strongest of sons!
They must knock down all the trees standing against me!"
Each day, with Northwind, he drove them into the ocean
To harden their bodies, shaking with fever.
Each day he watched them wrestle with saplings,
Panting and grunting, wrenching but not breaking.

"Stronger!" Ice shouted. He doused them with freezing water
And made them run with rocks lashed to their feet
Till his sons were weak and angry—all but Moss.
Moss grew in a corner of his father's house
And would not stand in the ocean or trudge with stones.
His brothers were jealous. They said, "Moss is afraid."

Moss said, "I have no enemies." Ice shouted,
"If you have no enemies, you have no father!"
And he scattered Moss into the deepest woods
Where he lay down at the feet of the great trees
On the side of Northwind, in rain and snow,
And, with strong arms, wrestled with them forever.

How Stone Held His Breath

Ice shouted, "My sons are stealing my breath!"
From among them, he picked Stone
And squeezed him whiter than Moon,
Ground him on cliffsides, dragged him down canyons.

"See what becomes of thieves!" Ice shouted
And pitched him through crackling rivers,
Dropped him into the hard nest of his mouth
And gnawed him with hailstones.

Ice herded his other sons up mountains.
Under four winds, under the spilled rain,
Under the red foxtail of Sun,
Stone lay still, holding his cold breath.

The Boy Who Became Seagull

Ice tore the People's nets. "Give me my fish!" he shouted,
And took their salmon and sturgeon, broke them and ate them,
And broke canoes. He wrapped his bony wife
In those torn nets and filled her spruce-root basket
With mussels and crabs, chitons and limpets.

That gray-faced wife walked through the silent village
Where the People had nothing. She would smile through doorways,
And the People would weep. She carried that basket always,
But she had teeth like Ice, and no one touched it.
The People were starving. Ice shouted, "Give me your bones!"

That boy was hungry. His mother gave him fishtails
And empty barnacles, clams filled only with water,
The broken lodges of rock snails full of sand,
The skins of ribbon worms, spongeweed and sea bats,
Pieces of coral. He ate them and grew strong.

He ate the feathers of seabirds and fishscales,
He ate the foam on the shore, he ate sea-fog,
He ate the gray-and-white daylight of winter,
He ate Northwind, and out of his thin, hard shoulders
He sprouted gray-and-white wings. Now he was Seagull.

Ice crouched at the mouth of the river. "Feed me!" he shouted.
And Seagull flew, screaming for all the People,
And plucked the eyes of Ice, cracked them and ate them,
And Ice turned over and broke to many pieces
And floated out to sea, melting and weeping.

And Hunger, his wife, followed, spilling her basket.

Devil's Club

That boy was lonely. He said, "Who was my father?"
His mother said, "His name was drowned in the river."
He went to the riverbank with his strong bow,
Angry, meaning to kill that water,
But River said, *Your father is still breathing.*

Again he said, "What was my father's name?"
She said, "Ghosts have no names. He was killed by Alder."
He went to Alder with his ax, meaning to bite it
As deep as Beaver, but Alder told him,
I have not fallen. Your father is still standing.

He said, "My father is breathing! He is still standing!"
She said, "He fought against Rock, and Rock crushed him."
That boy sharpened his knife and stabbed at Rock
Till the blade was broken. Rock said, *I am sitting*
Still to dream like your father. He is beside you.

Devil's Club grew in the shadow of Rock and Alder
By River, his body crooked and thorny.
That boy sat dreaming under his broad leaves
And red berries. He was not lonely. His thorns
Thickened in that dream, and his roots deepened.

His body grew long and crooked, and Blue Grouse
Came to his thin shoulders, drumming and feeding.
He grew as tall as his father, deep in shadows,
Swaying in rain, leaning far over water,
And his mother lay between them like Moss-Weeping.

How Stump Stood in the Water

Ice had many sons. "Find me my food!" he shouted.
They searched in the air and under the water
And brought him Quail and Mussel, Goose and Oyster,
Blue Teal and Rock Crab, Widgeon and Salmon.

"More! More!" Ice shouted. "My sons must feed me!"
Some climbed after Eagle and fell. Some paddled
After Gray Whale and drowned. Some offered
Buzzard and Minnow, Coot and Sea Slug.

But Stump stood in the ocean, catching nothing.
"Foolish Stump!" Ice shouted. "What are you standing on?
What are you holding in your shut hands?
Feed me! Feed me!" But Stump said, "Father,

What am I standing on? What am I holding?
If you tell me, they will be yours forever."
Ice shouted, "You are standing on Flounder!
You have stolen the last sweet eggs of Killdeer

For your selfish dinner! The tide is rising!
Who brings me nothing will come to nothing!"
Then Ice pulled back his other sons to the north,
And the water rose, and the water ebbed away,

And on the barren shore, Stump stood alone
On his own feet, holding his life in his hands.

How Stump Found His Village

Stump went from lodge to river, the loud one,
From woods to swamp, the stone-thrower, stick-jabber,
Thief of all eyes and ears, wanting to stand
Where anyone else was standing, wanting no one
To hide from him, no one to be alone.

If someone breathed, Stump wanted that same air.
If someone drank, Stump wanted that water.
If someone dreamed, Stump wanted that whole dream in his belly.
He wanted the sharp teeth of Weasel, Magpie's feathers,
Wanted to wear the long quick skin of Blue Racer.

Weasel said, "Reeds, Reeds, whisper to Stump."
Magpie said, "Reeds, call Stump away
Through the green sunlight falling under your fingers."
Blue Racer said, "East Wind, lead Stump to a different village,"
And the Reeds whispered, "Yes!" and the East Wind, "Yes!"

Stump said, "Where are you, Weasel?" searching the swamp
And "Where are you, Magpie?" fighting the tall Reeds
And "Come quick, Blue Racer!" parting the thick stalks,
But the Reeds said, "Hush!" and "Here!" and "Over here!"
And East Wind, weaving, said, "There! Look there!"

Stump trampled the Reeds and swept them down with a stick,
Uprooted them, looked over and under, walked miles
And still saw Reeds and Reeds. He plucked a fistful,
Shouting, "Why have you hidden my People?
They belong to me! You are nothing!"

"Throw stones at me," said East Wind. "Stand where we stand,"
Said the Reeds, "we will keep you, we will listen forever."
"Breathe all of me," said East Wind. "Dream what we dream,"
Said the Reeds. "We too have teeth and wings," said East Wind,
"Come, wear the long quick skin of the moon."

Stump felt afraid. He heard the East Wind whisper,
"Weasel, Magpie, Blue Racer, for all the People,
Asked us to show you how to find your village.
This way! This is the way!" And in the dying evening
Stump entered his dark village, the lodges empty.

How Stump Fished in the Black River

Stump said, "I will fish in the Black River."
He stole Black Whale's tooth, sinew from Black Bear,
A branch from Black Locust, and Black Spider's
Longest thread, spun between moon and moon.

But the People said, "No! No one must fish there,
Not even Loon or Fish Hawk. No one knows
What lives under that water." Stump answered,
"I will catch and eat what no one has ever seen."

He called Fish Hawk and Loon. "I will teach you
To scream my name: He-Catches-the-Soul-of-the-River."
From Loon's swift breast, from Fish Hawk's hovering tail
He pulled black feathers and thrust them into his hair.

And he cast his hook far over the current
Where it ran darkest like the river of clouds
From the black throat of Northwind in the winter
And waited, singing, "Now I shall find my power."

He felt his hook hold still. Slowly the thread
Went down and down, slipped through his straining fingers
Sharply and keenly till the end slid under water
Where no one could catch it, then or ever.

And Stump crouched in the shallows, his hands bleeding.

How Stump Dreamed of Earthmaker

Stump said, "I must dream of Earthmaker."
Three days and nights he fasted and dreamed
Everything under the earth: the melted and lost
Sun of the Stone River, Copper Root, Flint Man
Whose tongue goes straight for the soul, Black Fire
And Slate Bird flying together under granite.

"No!" Stump said. "I must have Earthmaker
Here in my heart's eye." And he dreamed
Everything on the earth: Old Running Moss
And Thorn Foot racing with green shadows,
Skull Cup, Man-Inside-Out hunting his lost thumb,
The claws of Rat shaking the bonebush.

Stump cried, "Earthmaker! Earthmaker! The People say
No one has ever dreamed you." And he dreamed
Everything over the earth: Rainbow Man
Bent high across water, the burning feathers
Of Kingfisher gathered from the Land of the Dead,
Ice Tooth, Broken Cloud, Snake-Falling-Forever,

And went on dreaming into the heart's thicket
Till he saw Raven crack the egg of the sun
And Blue Wolf break the long bones of the moon,
Till he dreamed the five wrong names of Death.
The sky came close and huge. At last, Earthmaker
Loomed over him like the face of the First Darkness.

Stump said, "Now I have dreamed you. Now I look
Into your face. Now you shall make me wise."
And suddenly like a mouth the great mask
Opened, and took him in, and closed its teeth,
And Stump became a dream of Stump
In the heart of Earthmaker whose face no man can know.

How She-Cannot-Speak Ran Away

She was too shy, even at picking berries.
Her hands were too big, she would drop them,
She would drop her basket, the bushes grew
Too close together, her feet would catch in brambles,
She was too tall to reach them without kneeling,
Her mouth was too wide to open without grinning,
So she closed it. They called her She-Cannot-Speak.

When the People laughed, she would go away
Into the woods, crouching and hiding,
Being small and hard, wishing to live like Stone,
Good only at sitting, who needs nothing
To prove he is Stone, who says nothing.
While she crouched one day, not being clumsy,
Not fat, not wide-mouthed, Grizzly Bear found her.

He stood on his hind legs. He was Walks-Like-a-Man,
Cross-Foot-Whose-Name-Must-Not-Be-Spoken,
Small Eyes, Drop-Jaw. He looked at her.
He said, "You must sleep in a dark circle."
He said, "I will show you what to follow."
He said, "Tomorrow you will not remember."
He said, "I know the place where nothing changes."

And she went with him and stayed with him
And slept with him, helped him pick berries
With her thick fingers, and Grizzly Bear said nothing
When she stumbled against him or spilled her basket,
Said nothing when she hid her mouth with her hands.
But he brought strange meat. She would not eat it.
At night, while he slept, she heard somebody weeping.

She found a woman lying inside a cave
Who was half stone, who could not move her body.
That woman said, "Grizzly Bear brings strange meat:
Eat only its shadow. He wants you to be Stone.
You must run away. He wants you to sleep all winter."
That woman gave her a comb and some long hairs,
Hair oil and sand. She said, "These are a woman."

"The comb teeth say, *This is the way to turn.*
The long hairs say, *We know where to follow.*
The hair oil says, *Tomorrow I will remember.*
And the sand says, *I come from the heart of Changer.*"
She took them all and crept back to the hollow
Where Grizzly Bear lay sleeping his round sleep,
His snout the color of sleep, his fur like night.

She-Cannot-Speak stared long at Grizzly Bear
By moonlight: he was too big, too shy,
He was too tall and was always crouching,
His paws were too big, he was too clumsy,
The brambles caught at his fur, his mouth was too wide
And showed too many teeth, he would say nothing,
He brought strange meat. She began running away.

She ran, and he came after her, claws rattling,
And she threw down her comb. Looking back, she saw
Masses of dead trees spring out of the ground,
But Grizzly Bear picked his way between them
Like the eyes of Moon. He was not too fat
To follow her through fallen trunks and branches
Into a clearing, after her, after her.

She ran, throwing down long hairs turning to bushes
More closely woven than baskets, as tight
As cranberry thickets, but Grizzly Bear passed through
As easily as a wind. She poured out hair oil:
It turned to a broad lake shining between them,
And his teeth were shining as he ran around it
Sway-footed, swift, after her, after her.

She dropped the sand then. It swelled to a cliffbank
Too steep for claws, too loose for him to climb.
She stood at the top of it, he crouched at the bottom.
They stared at each other through the ragged blanket
Of dawn. She turned away, not shy, not hiding,
Not wanting to sit like Stone, her mouth
Coming open and open, ready to speak to the People.

How Lies-in-the-Water Became Seaweed

She had no sister. Her brothers would tease her
In the woods, in the cranberry marshes. They would touch her.
They would follow her, teasing. They would pull her hair,
So she cut it off and went to play in the sea.
They followed her. She swam out further and further,
As far as Fish-catcher, and would stay there,
Floating. They called her Lies-in-the-Water.

Her father wanted the head of Jellyfish
To hang in the lodge. Then she would harm no one
While her blood was rising under its first moon.
So her brothers took their canoes out far, out far
Where the sea shines by itself, even at night,
Where the sea burns without the firebows of stars.
They found long hair uncoiling in the swells.

They followed it. They came to a fiery head
Gleaming beneath them, swelling and shrinking.
They cut that hair with their knives. They took that head
Burning in their hands. Their hands were burning
All the way to the lodge, and that head burned
All the next day on their sister's wall. She lay
Under it, safe and dangerous, dreaming her hair.

And her head was burning. It was swelling and shrinking.
She dreamed Sea Mother came to the cold shore.
Her huge white eyes opened and closed.
The shadows of seabirds circled her five fins.
She swelled and shrank. Her breath whitened the waves.
She cried, "Give me my daughter!" And hair from the head
Of Jellyfish on the wall grew back again.

It grew to the floor. It grew through the lodge doorway.
It grew to the sand. It grew into the water.
Lies-in-the-Water took that head in her arms
And walked the path of hair with her sister.
Her own lost hair grew longer, and Sea Mother
Took her head in her arms, took her away
That night, coiling her hair, to be Seaweed.

Loon

She would not speak to him. He was too poor,
He was still a boy, he was too small, too quiet,
There was too much darkness in his face,
He had no father, and she was the daughter
Of a dead chief. She lived alone and hungry.

He followed the river to a mountain lake
At night to die. He stared at the water,
Wanting to turn to nothing under it.
But out of the dark lake came the head of Loon
Staring at him, scattering copper moonlight.

Loon said, *You may wear my skin.* And he wore it.
His eyes and his beak were copper, around his neck
A ring of copper. He dove into the water
And fished all night for Trout. In the cold morning
He went as himself and laid it at her doorway.

While she cooked Trout, he heard her whispering,
"Heron has come with his gift. I will marry him."
And she ate all day. Now she was not hungry.
She combed her hair with Devil's Club, thinking
How her good father had come again as Heron.

He wore the skin of Loon at nightfall. He dove
And swam the white river, plunging and flying
More swiftly under the water than that water
Flying over the boulders, and caught Steelhead
And laid it dead at her doorway by morning.

While she cooked Steelhead, he heard her saying,
"Black Bear has brought his wealth. I will marry him."
And she ate till evening. Now she was full and happy.
She combed her hair with rose-thorns, knowing
Her rich dead father had come again as Black Bear.

He wore the skin of Loon into the sea
All the next night and fished in the kelp beds,
Rose into starlight, shaking and singing,
Then dove like Fish Hawk out of the wave-clouds
And brought King Salmon to the sill of her lodge.

She baked King Salmon, and he heard her boasting,
"Sea Lion wants my heart. I will marry him."
She ate all day, all night, and all morning
And combed her hair with Sea-Urchin, dreaming
Her father would fatten her like the wife of Sea Lion.

The skin of Loon became his. It would not come off.
He lifted his beak and stabbed it in saltwater,
He stretched his webbed feet, he stretched his foam-specked wings
And swam away into the rich sea,
Crying the long, thin, falling laughter of Loon.

Moon-Skin

No chief was great enough to be her husband.
Her rich mother and father guarded her
Aginst the fur-draped men who wanted her.
She held herself apart. She loved herself
More than those furs. She loved her body,
Seeing it shine in secret, dreaming inside it.

Each day she walked with her sisters in the woods,
Beautiful, safe, hidden among them,
Believing ferns unfolded only for her.
One day she found Slug on the path, his horns
Gleaming among her fernbeds. She kicked at him
And said, "You are only crawling like those others!"

That night in the lodge, while all her sleeping sisters
Guarded the foot of the ladder beneath her,
She lay awake, in love with her body.
And a young man stood beside her, his hair gleaming,
Silent and waiting. She touched his skin. It was smooth
And cold as Marten's fur under the water.

She lay with him. He held her body closer
Than her own skin had held it. She was shining
Like slowly melting hoarfrost against him,
Her eyes and lips were gleaming, he covered her
With the many skins of Moon, his mouth
Was hard, but it moved against her all that night.

When Sky Blanket trembled open, the young man whispered,
"Come stay with me in the lodge of my father."
She stole away with him by the first light,
Bringing only her body, feeling as safe
In her sleek skin as if surrounded by sisters,
Proud of the path glistening under their feet.

But his father's lodge was cold and damp. He left her
To lie down in the dark where water dripped,
Catching at sunlight through the cracks in the roof.
She saw Slug's body there, his wet horns shining,
His hard mouth opening, closing, even in sleep,
His belly oozing Moon-Skins without her.

Blindman

She fed her husband snow, that Blindman,
Put only snow in his dish, saying, "Snow
Is all we have to eat." She ate dried salmon
Outside their lodge, hoping Blindman would die.

Grizzly Bear came hunting along the river.
She was frightened. She ran, crying, "Blindman!
You must shoot Grizzly Bear!" She strung his bow
And drew his arrow for him, and Blindman shot.

His arrow sang through the heart of Grizzly Bear,
But she said, "Honey Snout is running away!
You have missed him, Blindman! You are too old and blind!"
She skinned that bear and cooked his meat in secret.

While she ate meat, Blindman ate only snow.
He had heard his arrow singing through the heart
Of Cross-Foot, and he said, "Bring me my arrow."
She threw it down beside him, and he smelled Bear.

That night he climbed through snow to Bitter Lake,
Finding the path through the storm inside his skull,
And the dark head of Loon came out of the water.
Blindman said, "I am blind. I want to die."

Loon said, "Lie down and weep." Blindman lay down
And wept, and out of his eyes came blood and smoke,
Ashes and hair and dust, and his eyes opened,
And he saw trees and water, snow and moonlight.

She came to find him, and he hid in the woods.
On the shore she found his blood, ashes, and hair,
And shouted, "Something has killed and eaten Blindman!"
She laughed and sang, running to cook meat.

His heart felt frozen. He was not old or hungry.
He walked to his empty lodge, smelling the smoke
Of that secret fire drifting along the river.
He barred his thick lodge door with stones and waited.

She came through the cold, full of her good dinner.
When she found the lodge door barred, she shouted, "Blindman!
You are dead and eaten!" Blindman said, "I will live."
She shouted, "I am cold!" He said, "I am not blind."

She shouted, "Be dead!" He said, "I am eating snow."
He waited all night, feeding his hungry eyes
On his hands and arrows. In the morning she was lying
Frozen in the snow, her white mouth filled with snow.

Woman-Asleep

Her husband said, "Who is stealing your soul?"
She said, "Northwind is rattling the trees."
Her husband loved her, but Woman-Asleep loved Rattle.
All day her husband watched her, and all night
She thought of that young Rattle without sleeping.

Her husband said, "Someone has tied his hair
Around a bone and thrown it against you."
She thought of Rattle filling her empty body
And said, "I am dying. Carve my burial box
And tie it in the branches of Cedar."

Her husband carved it, and she pretended to die.
Weeping, he lashed her high in that broken tree.
All day and all night her husband sang to her.
On the third night, she scraped hornspoons with a knife
And let the shavings drop on him like maggots.

He went away to mourn, and Woman-Asleep
Called out to Rattle from her burial box.
He came in the night and lay with her. Each night
He would untie her box and lie with her. She would sleep
All day alone as if in her own lodge.

One night her husband, his face still blackened with pitch,
His hair still burnt, came back, singing beneath her.
He sang, "Woman-Asleep, you are only sleeping,
You are only dreaming." And Northwind began blowing.
It sang, *Woman-Asleep, you will never waken.*

Old-Mother-Who-Cannot-Close-Her-Eyes
Lived under that Cedar, her thin voice creaking
Whenever Northwind blew. That night she creaked,
Woman-Asleep and Rattle will be falling
Asleep together now. They will never waken.

Northwind blew at the ropes Rattle had loosened,
Howled till the box fell down out of the branches
And broke beside the husband who sat singing,
"Woman-Asleep, why are you still sleeping?"
But Woman-Asleep and Rattle slept forever.

How Raven Stole Light

The People lived in darkness without Stars,
Unable to hunt or fish, as quiet as ghosts,
But Raven knew where Sun and Moon were hidden.
He flew through a sky as dark as his own feathers
And found a lodge surrounded by daylight.

A great chief lived there with his only daughter.
She came to their water-hole, and Raven changed
Into a hemlock needle floating across it.
She drank him, and he grew and grew inside her
Till she lay down on moss and Raven was born.

That chief doted on Raven: his black eyes gleamed,
His beak and tongue were quick, he would play with furs
And bundles of dried light. But Raven saw,
High at the ceiling, three shut bentwood boxes
And knew what they held. He began crying and crying.

They gave him deer-hoof rattles and crowberries,
But still he cried and pointed at those boxes.
They gave him shells and the sweet backbones of salmon,
But he cried and pointed, so the chief brought down
The Box of Stars and gave it to Raven.

He opened it, and there, like herring eggs,
The Stars glistened in clusters, and Raven laughed,
Tossing them through the smoke-hole where they tumbled
Across the sky forever. The chief was angry
And closed that smoke-hole, scolding at Raven.

So Raven cried for days and would eat nothing,
Would play with nothing, pointing at those boxes.
His eyes turned many colors. He squealed. His mother
Feared he would choke and die, so the chief took down
The second box and gave it to Raven.

He opened it, and Moon gleamed like a fire,
Like pitch-wood burning, like burning candlefish.
He rolled that Moon around the floor of the lodge,
Singing and laughing, but then he cried again
And pointed to the last box on the ceiling.

Closing his ears, the chief brought down that box,
And Raven took it, seizing Moon in his beak,
Broke through the smoke-hole, rolled Moon in the sky,
Opened the Box of Sun for the ghostly People,
And flew among them, scattering daylight.

How Raven Came to the Feast

The People had eaten nothing but barnacles
All that moon, whelks and halibut bones.
But now they had cakes of cranberries, salmonberries,
And the inner bark of hemlock to feast on.

The People said, "But what shall we tell Raven?
If he knows we have these cakes, he will eat too many!"
The People shouted, "Raven, come eat barnacles!
Eat bones again!" So Raven slept in his tree.

But Hawk from a gray sky-cliff saw them feasting
And stooped to tell Raven, and Raven was angry.
He hollowed rotten logs into canoes
And lined them with spruce cones standing down the middle.

To all those standing cones he stuck grass spears.
He pierced them with the feathers of Loon and Eagle
And blades of peach-leaf willow and hauled those logs
To the shore and set them floating toward the village.

And the People saw war canoes! War canoes coming!
Warriors with shaking helmets and spears shaking
And paddles stabbing the water like Kingfishers
And Whales' eyes on the prows and foaming teeth!

And the People ran away to the marshes, hiding,
And Raven ate their cakes, snapping his beak.
He heaped up empty whelk shells and halibut bones
In every lodge, then flew off cawing and cawing.

How Raven Stole Beaver's Pond

Raven said, "That Beaver is rich, he has many crayfish,
His pond is filled with trout, he has berries
Weighing their branches down into his mouth,
And frogs wait at his lodge door to be eaten."

So Raven dressed himself in his poorest feathers
And went to Beaver's lodge. He said, "I am poor,
I am your brother, we had the same father,
Show me your rich pond, we must eat together."

And Beaver took him to the water's edge
Where alder and cottonwood, maple and willow
Grew in young groves and peeled him the inner bark,
Bit off the pale-green shoots of waterlilies.

While Beaver gnawed at them, he said, "Good brother,
Why do you hide your hands under those feathers?
Your feet look crooked and sore. Your two black teeth
Look old and hollow. I must chew these for you."

When Raven saw those crayfish and trout and frogs
Swimming beyond him, the ripest berries hanging
Over the water where he could not reach them,
He scowled at the sticks and twigs heaped for his dinner.

He shouted, "Beaver is greedy! Beaver is no brother!
Yellow Teeth cannot fly! He is fat and muddy!"
He folded that pond together like a blanket
And carried it in his beak to a high firtree.

Beaver said, "No! Without it my good brothers
Raccoon and Muskrat, Marten, Bear, and Otter
Could not livë. You must give it back!" But Raven
Shook his head till rain shook out of the pond.

So Beaver gnawed at that firtree, gnawed a ring
Deep through its bark, deep through the white wood.
Raven shook harder. The firtree fell like thunder,
And Raven flew, spilling the pond on Beaver.

Cloud-Watcher

They disobeyed Cloud-Watcher, took their canoe too far,
And Southeast caught them, filled them with seafoam,
Broke wave after wave across them like trees falling,
And the forest sank in the sea behind them,
The mountains sank till nothing but strange water
Twisted them, turned their prow into the fog.

Cloud-Watcher said, "There!" and pointed. His four brothers
Said, "No! You will feed us to Sea Mother!
You will feed us all like fish to Man-Underneath!
We should go there or there!" They pointed paddles
Crosswind and downwind, into the mouth of wind,
Then jabbed their angry fingers at Cloud-Watcher.

The sea grew shallow. Beneath, Cloud-Watcher saw
Giant Anemone clinging to Fur Seal,
Holding it up to them like a gift. His brothers
Paddled and shouted, "Sea Monster will eat us!"
But Cloud-Watcher sang the song of Anemone,
Thanking her as she sank, leaving them nothing.

They saw gray rocks and beached themselves and ate
Sea-mist for days. They spit their hearts at Cloud-Watcher.
Again, he said, "There!" and pointed. They said, "No!
You will drown us! You will feed us to Southeast!"
One brother died of thirst, one froze in his sleep,
One starved, one screamed and ate too many stones.

Then Cloud-Watcher sat alone in the wind. The body
Of Fur Seal drifted ashore to die beside him.
He wore its skin and stared through its deep eyes,
And mountains and forests rose out of the water
Where he had pointed. He set his brothers' bones
Upright in that canoe, steering them homeward.

The bones went rowing there, fearless and singing.

Fireweed

Burnt Forest hid his daughter. He kept her
Hidden among the black stumps of his lodge.
She was called Fireweed. She belonged to him.
Young men would sing to her, but she would listen
With one ear always turned to her father.
Young men would go to her and would vanish.

Cloud-Watcher came to that lodge full of his power.
He wanted Fireweed, so he turned to ashes
And drifted at night down through the smoke-hole
And lay with her in the shape of Cloud-Watcher.
But while they were still asleep in the morning,
Burnt Forest hovered over them like a stormcloud.

He said, "My son-in-law, I am cold and weak.
You must go to Black Mountain. You will see an alder.
You must cut it down and bring it for my lodge fire."
So Cloud-Watcher went to that mountain with his ax
And struck that alder and fell into darkness,
Fell deep into his mind and disappeared.

He was inside that tree. It held him hard
In its pale heartwood, but Cloud-Watcher called his power
And burst it open like a splintering doorway.
Out of it poured splinters of young men's bones,
Their broken bodies. He took that tree on his shoulder
To the lodge door of Burnt Forest and set it afire.

Burnt Forest said, "Son-in-law, I see you.
Now I am hungry. Go down to the Black Sands
And catch me Devilfish to cook for my dinner."
So Cloud-Watcher went to the shore and fished
With a crooked hemlock root among the rocks.
He felt a tug, and his mind plunged under water.

He was inside Devilfish, gripped by its belly.
He called his power and burst it. Out of its beak
Came pouring half-eaten pieces of young men.
He dragged that carcass back to the alder fire
And cooked it black. Then Fireweed glanced at him,
Half-turned to her father, half-listening, half-smiling.

Burnt Forest said, "Now you may take my daughter.
You may have my canoe. It is full of grease and berries."
A rotten log with roots lay in the water,
But Cloud-Watcher carried Fireweed into it
And said, "Fly home, my canoe!" It started moving.
It filled with berries and grease. Its prow became Heron.

Behind them, seething in clouds on the black shore,
Burnt Forest shouted, "Give me back my daughter!"
And Heron turned its neck. The canoe was turning.
Cloud-Watcher sang, feeding it grease and berries
Till it flew forward, but slowly Fireweed withered
To small gray seed-crowns flying back to her father.

How Southeast Came to the Dancing House

They were there in the dancing house, those spirits,
They came there: Devilfish trailing his many arms,
From his beak a song coming slowly out of hiding
Like his dark cloud spilling toward the People,
A suddenly quick song between rocks, shaking the floor,
Then no song, no song.

And Hanging Hair, as thick and green as a thicket,
Grown long as night, shedding her red flowers,
Swelling and ripening, her song the color of blood
Turned sweet as the sharp thorns crossing her mouth.
Oh, the People's mouths opened and opened,
And the walls shook as if remembering trees.

And Crooked Beak, cloud-biter, eater of Lightning Snake,
Percher on Thunder, his wings crossing Sun and Moon,
Star-breaker, his song like the splitting of bones,
A whistle through lost marrow, and the smoking roof
Shaking and shaking for the People.
Then through the door's mouth came Killer Whale.

His fin was scraping the rooftree, his song a death song
As he lay down to be eaten. But after him poured black tides
Choking with seaweed, and black clouds blowing black rain,
Black snow and hailstones, and Devilfish sliding
Through the floor, Hanging Hair flowing through wall planks,
And Crooked Beak flapping away through the ceiling.

And the Post of Heaven was shaking,
The People were shaken till they heard their souls
Rattle in their clenched bodies,
And out of the wind came the screaming of Southeast:
"Come home, my brother!" And Killer Whale swam out
Toward his deep storm-lodge, leaving the People hungry.

How Canoe-Maker Fought with Southeast

Canoe-maker said, "I must fight Southeast,
That father of bad weather!" With adze and wedges
He carved a war canoe with a high prow,
With the eyes and great fin of Killer Whale,
But Southeast sent out waves and broke it.

Three times he broke canoes. Canoe-maker felt wilder
Than any weather. He toppled a whole cedar
Into that gray water, riding among the branches
Toward Southeast and lifting his harpoon
Like a chief with a speaker's staff shaking his spirit.

Canoe-maker said, "I know where you lie! I see you!"
And he struck deep through tangles of seaweed
Where Southeast lived, now darkened with anger.
Oh, he called all his sons to fight Canoe-maker,
And they came flying, tumbling over each other:

Stormcloud low to the water with those winds
Breaker-of-Treetops and Pebble-rattler
And then Thick Sea-mist. Canoe-maker sang for his power
And clung to the branches, his body beaten
Pale as a shell, pale as the sky's teeth.

But the last son, Tidal Wave, rose and covered him
Like a green hillside breaking with gray flowers
And carried him ashore, locked with that cedar,
And left him to shake in Southeast's fingers
Like a storm rattle, white as the driftwood.

Wild Man

He nearly drowned getting firewood from that island,
His canoe broken by Northwind, his ax broken,
And his dog drowned, his good dog,
His dog sleeping now where he made fire
Under hemlock branches, but he did not sleep himself
For fear Land Otters would turn him to Wild Man.

On the third night of watching and watching,
He skinned that dog and wore him over his shoulders
And wore the head on his head. Now he could smell
Everything in the dark, he could see in the dark,
He had many teeth. He sharpened one narrow legbone
And waited for Land Otters, drinking nothing.

Old Man came to the fire, Young Woman, Shadow People,
All carrying baskets of mussels and barnacles.
They set them down, but he was too cunning.
When no one looked, he stabbed them with that legbone:
It sank as if through fog. He poured their baskets
Into the fire: wood lice and ants ran, burning.

They vanished. They could not trick him. He was not Wild Man.
The head on his head was snarling after them,
And dog's blood flowed in his mouth. His claws grew.
He would never sleep again. He would eat and drink
Nothing, not even leaves, not rain, not sunlight,
Not darkness. Those Land Otters would not catch him.

In the third week he saw the canoe landing.
His father, his mother, his wife had come to save him,
But they were frightened by the power of his dog skin.
He sniffed and snarled. He knew they were Land Otters.
They tried to touch him. He stabbed at them with that legbone,
But they gripped him in their arms as if they were People.

The skull on top of his skull began howling.

The Man Who Killed Too Many

No one could make harpoons like Wood-carver.
They would sing in the air or under the water
Like Goldeneye or Surf Scoter.
They would swim back to his hands like his children
And bring him Sea Lion and Sea Otter.
He would stand on the reef all day, singing and killing,
But he killed too many, and the People were angry.

The People said, "He will kill them all!
We shall go hungry!" So they stole his canoe
And abandoned him. Wood-carver sat on the reef,
And Sea Lion and Sea Otter were silent.
His harpoons fell silent. Nothing was singing
In the air, in the water. He sat alone,
As cold as their salt blood. He began to die.

Grebe swam to his side, saying, *Wood-carver,
The Chief asks you to come*, and it dove
Deep into the sea, and Wood-carver dove deeper
Than his harpoons without thinking or speaking
And found himself in the lodge of Killer Whale
Whose floor-planks were white bone, whose roof was nothing,
And Killer Whale said, *Why do you kill my People?*

Wood-carver felt afraid. Other harpoons
Lay broken at his feet, their iron beaks
No longer parted, flying, singing their death songs.
From high on the house-post, Killer Whale
Brought down his fin and pressed it to Wood-carver.
It grew on his back. He was shaken like a rattle
Deep in that water, and he took his power.

He dreamed he was in the stomach of Sea Lion,
Rising and floating. He woke. He was ashore
Near his own village. He saw his wife still mourning,
Her hair burnt off, her face covered with pitch,
Hungry, his children hungry, the People hungry.
All day he carved killer whales out of cedar
And painted their bellies white as that lodge floor.

He took those whales to the sea and floated them
With the ebbtide, saying, "Grandfather, .
I will carve nothing but you. Let your People
Bring themselves to us when they wish to die."
And the carved whales swam back in the morning
With Rock Cod, Salmon, and Halibut in their mouths,
And Wood-carver brought his knives again to the village.

Wood-Carver and Cedar Woman

His wife died young. Wood-carver mourned for her.
He hid far in the woods and sang her death
Night after night, and Cedar mourned with him
And died and fell. With his sharp adze
Day after day Wood-carver shaped her body,
Her face, her fingers, then carried her to his lodge
And set her like herself at the blanket-loom.

He painted her with the blood of flowers and roots.
He would speak to her. He would answer for her,
Calling himself He-Breathes-for-the-First-People,
He-Wears-the-Skin-of-Dogfish, He-Stares-Through-Wood,
Stone Drum, Breaker-of-Many-Branches, Stump,
He-Sits-in-Circles, He-Dreams-in-the-Heart-of-Trees.

But the People heard two voices in that lodge.
They said, "Wood-carver has split himself in two!"
They stole his adze, his wedges, his bent knives
For fear he would carve them, for fear he would split them all,
Hunting his wife in the heartwood of their bones.

Wood-carver sat by Cedar Woman. He sang,
"Again she gathers the wool of Mountain Goat!
She weaves the feathers of Eagle, the black claws
Of Grizzly Bear, the yellow mouth of Sea Monster!"

The People hid, but they heard Wood-carver singing,
"Her roots are growing into the lodge floor!
She drinks from the opening eyes of Earthmaker!"

He sang, "Once more she hears He-Sings-to-Trees!
She speaks to him again like Voice-Out-of-Cedar!"

And she started weaving her unfinished blanket.

How Fish-Catcher Lost His Salmon

He wove that trap with its wings flying downstream,
But nothing came to the weir of Fish-catcher.
He fasted and sang, but Salmon stayed in the sea.
He said, "I must marry a ghost to help me."

He went to Grave-of-Stones and said, "Dead Woman,
Come out of your stones and bring me Salmon."
She came, her round eyes staring at him and shining.
Her blanket was green and silver. He married her.

She split long spruce roots and wove a basket,
Then walked into the river, staring and singing.
She sang like rain on leaves, like snow-melt
Falling in milky pools, and Salmon came.

They filled the weir, she filled her basket, they leaped
And fought in Fish-catcher's arms, and he killed them.
He said, "You must die, my Salmon, and feed me!"
He split them on drying-racks by the riverside.

She sang, and they came and came. Fish-catcher said,
"You must dry in the sun!" He laughed, lifting his knife.
They stared at him and fought while he split them.
He shouted, "You are nothing but ghosts to be eaten!"

Dead Woman waded upstream and broke his trap,
Spilling her basket. She swam under the water,
Leaving Fish-catcher, and Salmon leaped
Down from their racks, after her, toward the mountains.

The Burial of Salmon-Flying

He could not name what he wanted. He dreamed he would find it
In Salmon's nest, but his mother and father told him
He must not go where Salmon drums with her tail,
Then dies on the stones of the river. He went there.

He saw Fish Hawk and Eagle, Gull and Crow
Diving on Salmon. They would soar and scream,
Then dive to tear her copper-and-silver side
And eat her flesh and feast on her lost children.

He brought a stone covered with Salmon's eggs
In secret to the lodge. His mother and father
Had nothing for him to eat, and he was hungry.
At night in the fire he heated that nesting stone.

While he leaned over it, dreaming, it broke open
Like Salmon spawning. It covered his body
With hard, black, burning eggs from the ghost of Salmon.
He sat all night and all day and would eat nothing.

He sat three days, and the People came to him
With roots and water, but his eyes and mouth stayed shut.
His mother and father bathed him, but he sat silent.
On the fourth night, his body walked to the river.

He followed it upstream to the white valleys,
Dropping his blankets. Now he was dead. His eyes
Were open, his mouth would open, but his body
Was not his body. It was thick with scales and feathers.

He spread his fins and swam to the Tree of Morning,
Leaped to the highest branches where West Wind
Carries its cloudy river against the mountains
To spawn white hailstones, churning and drumming.

He dove and danced in West Wind, swimming the air
Where the People were fishing. They saw Salmon-Flying
With the face of a man. He flew to a hemlock,
Perched, and sang, *You must lie down in the water.*

They felt afraid, they ran, but he followed, singing,
You must dance to Salmon's drum on her stony nest.
They hid in the village. He sat on his father's lodge
And sang, *You must build my nest under the stones.*

The People made his nest while he soared above them,
Watching and screaming. Then he dove like Fish Hawk
And let himself be taken. The People touched him.
His mother and father closed his claws and his fins.

They put him in that lodge, shutting its roof
Forever under stones. The People lay down
And sang in the water, then rose and danced
To the cold clear drum of Salmon under the river.

7. The Songs of He-Catches-Nothing

He-Catches-Nothing

He-Catches-Nothing built his lodge of driftwood
At the end of the village where the People threw
Fishheads and fishtails to the dogs. They saw him
Moving alone and thin each evening
To get his share after those strong dogs
And boil his soup, the color of seawater.

Each morning he would fish, singing for luck
With the others, but his canoe had lost its eyes,
His kelp-line was too thick, his halibut-hook
Was only spruce teeth, boneless, he owned no water
By the good shoals where the People had named them
After their fathers. He fished in empty places.

One day, his hook held still. Fish-catcher shouted,
"He has caught the bottom of the sea! Let him take it
Home to his lodge and boil it for dinner!"
The People laughed. He-Catches-Nothing pulled,
Calling his only hook back to his hands,
But it came slowly as light in the morning.

The People helped him, laughing at his thick kelp,
And hauled till their splashing was like seagulls,
Heaving and bobbing. They hauled, their prows awash,
While under the sea, wider than ten canoes,
They saw the gleaming, glittering pale-pink mouth
Of Abalone Mother like Moon-Drowning.

Fish-catcher shouted, "She must wait for Fish-catcher!"
And the People shouted, "You must cut your line!"
He-Catches-Nothing cut his line, and slowly
Abalone Mother sank to her hiding place.
Again, the People fished. He-Catches-Nothing
Went to his lodge to wait behind the dogs.

Song Asking for Mercy from the Bushes

You know what you must be, you know
Where your roots are branching,
You have stood still to learn
The speech of Rain-Bringing Wind
And the silence of Cold-Bringer,
You know who comes to you,
Manzanita, dark-red berry-maker,
Deer-feeder, hider of Fox Sparrow,
And Dogbane whose shredded stems
Weave themselves to fishline,
Ninebark for Mountain Goat,
Arrow-wood whose stone quiver
Lifts plumes like sea-spray,
Buckthorn and Bitter Cherry
Where Woodpecker and Black Bear
Touch their claws together:
I walk among you, not sleeping,
Not knowing what I must be
Or where my roots are hiding,
Not knowing the speech of rain
Or the signs of Snow Moon,
But among your silent leaves
Saying your true names
And begging: tell me my own.

Song After Fasting in a Tree

I had watched for it in a sky
Thickened by Moon's held breath
Or out of the turning ground
Below me, dim as my hands,
Or from ash leaves restless as eyelids
Or out of the dog-circling wind,
But my spirit came
On the third night from no direction,
Not up through the hollow tree
But from my heart's hollow.

Now my throat and my breast
Grow mottled like ash bark,
My beak darkens and hardens,
My feathers lengthen, I fall
Forward, gliding silent on wings,
Seeing the least quiver of grassblades
Even where branches catch their own shadows
In the Dance of the Broken Claws, I fall
Again, deeper, and my fast is ended
Now, with you, Mouse-brother.

Song from the Roof of a Flooded Lodge

Be afraid, you chiefs! Here is your chief, rich Tidal Wave,
One-Furthest-Ahead, Great Canoe-Breaking Dancer!
He throws away his property without looking behind him!
He brings Man-Underneath-the-Sea rolling out of his forehead!
He scatters Kelp and Seaweed, he fills the bowls of your lodges
And sits at his ease among you, the strugglers shouting for gifts,
The little chiefs who have come, empty-bellied, to his potlatch,
Who now are filled with him, whose ears roar with his praise,
Whose mouths must drink the songs of Abalone and Mussel
In his honor, the slow songs, the endless songs of saltwater!

Song After Being Abandoned

They have taken all their dogs
Away with them to the mouth
Of Southeast-Sleeping,
Have emptied the whole village.
They think I will eat alone,
Growling at no one.
They think I will fish alone,
Still catching nothing.

But I call new People now
To a feast! Here on the shore
I call them, and they come
Floating. The white-and-clear pieces
Of the broken sons of Ice
Come floating. I carry them
One by one to my lodge.
I serve them dried berries.

I pour oil on the fire.
None will go hungry.
None will be cold.
Now we will sing new songs
And weep for our great pride.
Our bodies will shine
Like fish caught in a dream.
Then slowly we will lie down.

Song for the Death of Hummingbird

He flew in my sleep, that Hummingbird, Long-Tongue,
Copper Dancer, He-Whispers-to-Flowers,
He-Sits-on-the-Bush-of-Ghosts. I felt afraid,
And deep in my sleep, I killed him. When I woke,
He lay on the ground, eyes bleeding, his beak bleeding.

Now everywhere, the People are sleeping.
They lie in the sand or stiff in their lodges
Not moving, not speaking, the sea forgotten.
Their fires burn low, their canoes are drifting,
They lead He-Laughs-Behind into darkness.

I hold that empty bird
Toward the nest of Star-Claw,
Toward the broken shell of Sun,
Toward the moss cup of Moon,
Asking for his pardon.

The People sleep,
But I cannot sleep.
I am left on the shore
Between sand and wind
Between fire and rain.

I am waiting
For his answer.
I am awake,
But I dream
I am singing.

Song from the Lodge of the Shadow People

I am lying still in the lodge
Of the Shadow People, hearing
By the small cold fire
The song of the Game of Silence.

If I sleep through this night,
Not laughing or weeping,
Not shouting, not praying,
I will earn their gifts by morning:

Copper Forehead and Flint Heart,
The sinew of Winter Wren,
Their Dancing-Blanket woven
Of moss, leaves, and lichen,

Their necklace of Bighorn hoofs
So my shadow may climb home,
The legbones of Whistling Swan
Through which all ghosts drink rain.

When I wake, they will teach me
To hold still and to vanish.
Who hears me will see No One
In this empty lodge, singing.

Song of a Man Who Rushed at the Enemy

I could have fought like Fox who can see behind him,
Who can bite even while running away, or like Owl
Who will hide deep in his hollow but will not surrender.

I could have fought like Snake who only waits to be told
Belong to this place where you are sleeping to stay quiet
But who strikes what comes toward him till he is broken.

But I must rush at my enemy like Bear Mother and Badger
Who know already how to sleep under the ground, or Wolverine
Who will not turn away, who will fight even with Earthmaker.

Now I am running on the shore toward the Iron People,
Toward their smoke and fire-sticks, against their spitting stones.
I am running faster than Dragonfly who needs to sing nothing.

I am running toward them on the shore forever, singing this.

Burial Song

My body ran on its legs and waved its hands,
Dug holes, cracked wood. It leaped into water,
Leaped out again, made fire, flinched from fire.
It climbed over rocks and hurried from one place to another
And came back to its beginning, aiming its empty ears
And eyes into the four mouths of the wind.
My body carried another body into the woods,
Forgot itself, found itself, lost itself.

Now it lies still. Children may tease it with sticks
Or women call to it, laughing behind their fingers,
Or men challenge it with their proud crowing,
But it wants nothing from them and will not move.
Its hands stay where they belong—together—
Its eyes shut, its heels not rising or dragging,
And its mouth keeping a cold council.

My body has stopped. Now yours will go forward,
But mine will stay in this Now, exactly here.
Tomorrow it will seem far behind you.
Though you squint till you weep, you will not see it
Nor will Hawk from the edge of his cloud
Nor will Owl see it in this different darkness.
Yet it will lie in wait for you to remember
Like a dream stiffened with danger.